3/17

FIRST SCIENCE EXPERIMENTS

EXPERIMENTS WITH LIVING THINGS

By Anna Claybourne

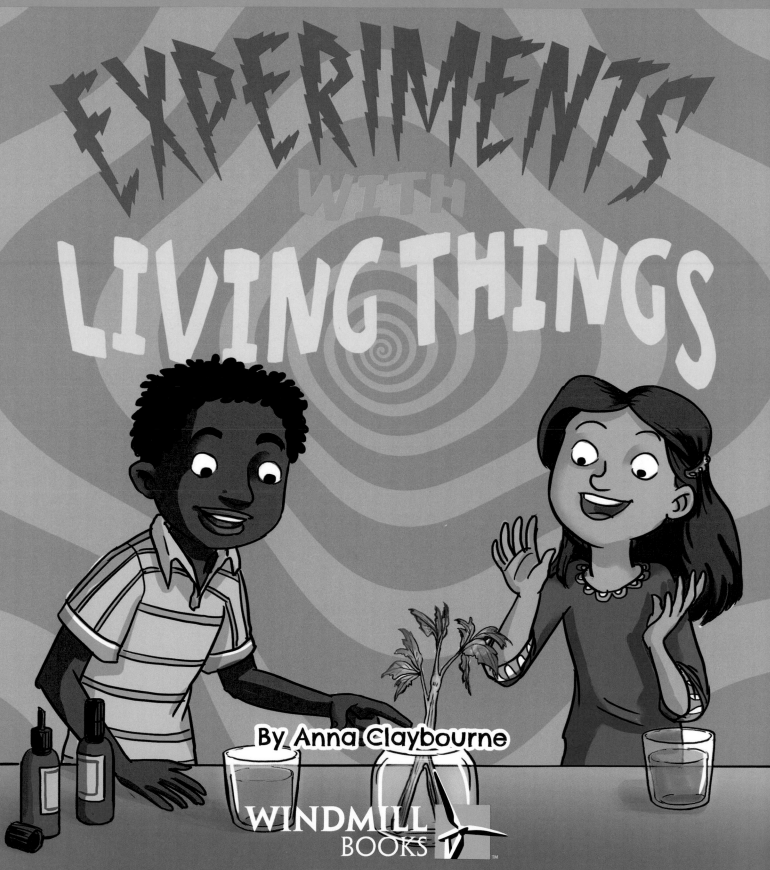

WINDMILL BOOKS ™

Published in 2017 by **Windmill Books**, an Imprint of Rosen Publishing
29 East 21st Street, New York, NY 10010

Author: Anna Claybourne
Designer: Emma Randall
Illustrations: Caroline Romanet

CATALOGING-IN-PUBLICATION DATA

Names: Claybourne, Anna.
Title: Experiments with living things / Anna Claybourne.
Description: New York : Windmill Books, 2017. | Series: First science experiments | Includes index.
Identifiers: ISBN 9781508192435 (pbk.) | ISBN 9781508192398 (library bound) | ISBN 9781508192312 (6 pack)
Subjects: LCSH: Plants--Experiments--Juvenile literature. | Biology--Experiments--Juvenile literature.
Classification: LCC QK52.6 C627 2017 | DDC 570'.78--dc23

Manufactured in the United States of America
CPSIA Compliance Information: Batch #BS16PK: For Further Information contact Rosen Publishing, New York, New York at 1-800-237-9932

Contents

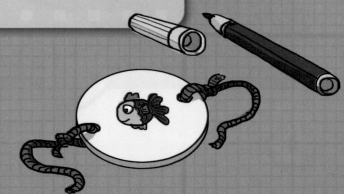

Living things

What makes you different from a coin, a spoon or a lump of ice? You're alive – an eating, breathing, growing, living thing. Our world is full of living things, from humans like you to huge whales, trees and flowers, dogs and cats, insects and tiny germs.

What are living things?

There are millions of different types of living things, and they are all different. But there are some things that all living things do...

THEY MOVE...

Plants lean towards the Sun.

People walk, run or dance.

THEY FEED...

Lions eat antelopes.

This toadstool feeds on a rotting tree stump.

THEY SENSE...

Plants sense light.

A shark sniffs out its prey.

THEY GROW...

You grow as you get older.

A sunflower grows very tall.

THEY MAKE MORE LIVING THINGS!

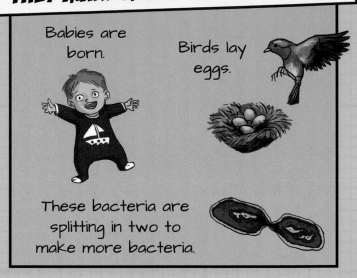

Babies are born.

Birds lay eggs.

These bacteria are splitting in two to make more bacteria.

Which is which?

The types of living things are called species. Each species is different and has its own name. The species can be divided into larger groups.

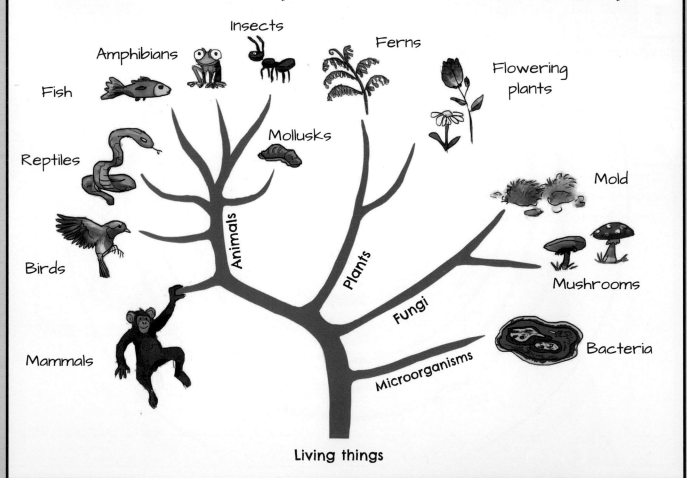

Insects

Amphibians

Fish

Ferns

Flowering plants

Reptiles

Mollusks

Mold

Animals

Plants

Birds

Fungi

Mushrooms

Mammals

Microorganisms

Bacteria

Living things

Grass caterpillar

Create your own caterpillar, and watch it grow grassy hair! This experiment lets you see how plants grow.

1 Mix a handful of grass seeds with several handfuls of compost. Cut off one leg of the tights, and pour the mixture in.

You will need:

- Grass seeds (from a garden center)
- Old pair of thin tights (not thick woolly ones)
- Scissors
- Rubber bands or hair bands
- Potting compost
- Googly eyes
- Watering can
- Old tray or plate

2 Tie the leg closed at the open end. Snip it off neatly. Stretch three or four rubber bands around the caterpillar to divide it into sections and a head.

3 Stick some googly eyes on the head (or make your own using buttons or cardboard). Put the caterpillar on a tray or plate.

Another fun idea

What happens if you make a caterpillar, but leave it somewhere dark? What happens if you don't water it? Try these tests to see what conditions seeds need to grow properly.

4 Put the tray or plate with your caterpillar on it on a sunny windowsill. If it's spring or summer, it could go outside in a garden or on a balcony.

5 Water your caterpillar's body every day, making sure it stays damp. Soon its hair will start to appear! How long does it take to grow?

What has happened?

When the grass seeds have plenty of light, water and soil, they start to grow. They grow roots and long leaves, which look like furry hair.

Rainbow celery

Have you ever seen a plant with red or blue leaves? Here's a clever way to make a stick of celery change color. It will look like magic!

You will need:

- Sticks of celery with leaves
- Two small glasses
- Red and blue food coloring
- Water
- Kitchen scissors

1

Trim the bottom of a stick of celery so that it is about 6 inches (15 cm) long. Leave the leaves on.

2

Pour water into a glass so it is a third full. Add a small amount of food coloring.

3

Put the end of the celery into the liquid in the glass. Leave the glass in a safe place, where it won't be moved.

4

After one day, cut across the base of the celery with scissors. You will see lines of color rising up the stalk.

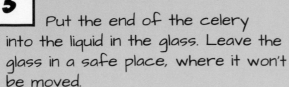

5

Put water and a small amount of food coloring in two glasses, one with red and one with blue. Split another stick of celery. Allow each part of the split stalk to stand in a glass.

6

On the following day, you will have rainbow-colored celery! Cut back the stalks to check.

What has happened?

Plants need water, just like we do. They take up water through their roots. The water travels in little tubes, all the way through the stem to the leaves. If you put dye in the water, the colored water will be carried to the leaves too!

Another fun idea

Put a flower with white petals in water with food coloring. Leave it overnight. What do you think will happen?

Dried fruit

There's one thing that all living things need, and that's water. In this experiment, you can find out just how watery plants are.

You will need:

- A selection of fruit, such as an orange, an apple, a peach and a banana
- A knife
- An oven
- A baking tray
- Weighing scales
- Pencil and paper

1

Weigh each fruit, and write down how much it weighs. Then slice up each fruit thinly. Spread slices out on the baking tray.

2 With an adult's help, put the tray in the oven. Set it to the lowest heat - usually about 225°F (100°C). Leave it for about 6 hours, or overnight.

3

Carefully take out the tray of dried-out fruit. Leave it to cool. Once cool, weigh each fruit again. How much less does each weigh?

What has happened?

Living things are made of tiny units called cells. Cells need water to make them work. Plants also take in water in order to make food and grow. A typical fruit is over 80% (or fourth-fifths) water. A human is a bit less watery – around 60-70%.

Flower photos

- A flower, such as a rose, poppy, carnation or daffodil, that is just starting to open (from your garden or a flower shop)
- A vase or jug of water
- A digital or smartphone camera
- A tripod, or some plasticine or sticky tack.
- A brightly lit room
- A computer

Take a series of flower photos to see how a flower opens its petals and blooms. You'll need to start in the morning, as it could take the whole day!

1 Stand your flower in the vase or jug of water. Set up your camera pointing at the flower. If you don't have a tripod, use plasticine or sticky tack to hold it still.

2 Take a photo of the flower every 20 or 30 minutes. Make sure you keep the lights on all day so it is easy to see.

3 Once the flower has opened, upload all your photos onto a computer. Arrange them in order of the time they were taken.

What has happened?

It's hard to see a flower opening, as it moves so slowly. But your photos let you see how it happens.

The rubbery bone

Bones are hard – aren't they? They hold your body up, and protect soft parts, like your brain. But you can make a bone go bendy and rubbery. Here's how!

You will need:

- A cooked chicken bone
- A plastic food container with a lid
- White vinegar
- Paper towels

1 First, you'll need to get your bone. The best way is to pull apart a well-cooked chicken leg. Take the bone out, and wash it well.

Try this!
Can you feel some of the hard bones in your body? Try feeling your head, cheeks, ankles and knees.

2 Put the bone in the container, then pour in enough white vinegar to cover it completely. Put the lid on tightly.

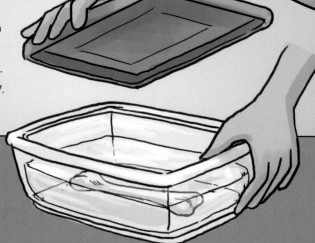

3

Leave the container somewhere safe for at least five days. Then open it, take the bone out, wash it and dry it with kitchen paper.

4

You'll find the bone has become rubbery and soft! Can you bend it in half? Can you tie a knot in it?

Did you know?

Dairy foods like milk and cheese contain calcium. That's why they are good for helping your body to grow strong bones and teeth. If you can't eat dairy foods, though, you can also get calcium from nuts, oranges, beans, sardines, and leafy vegetables like cabbage.

What has happened?

Animal bones – including your own – contain a mineral called calcium. It is what makes bones hard and strong. Vinegar is good at dissolving calcium. When it soaks into the bone, the calcium dissolves away. The softer, bendy parts of the bone are left behind.

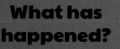

○ = calcium

Bone soaking in vinegar

Fly-eye glasses

Lots of animals have eyes. They use them to sense light, which helps them to tell where objects are. But not all eyes are the same. Make these glasses, and see the world through a fly's eyes!

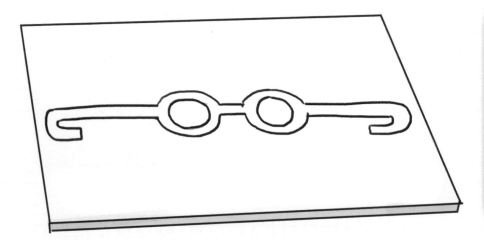

You will need:

· Card stock
· Marker
· Scissors
· Bubble wrap
· Glue or adhesive tape

1 Draw a pair of large round glasses onto the card stock, like this. Include the arms of the glasses sticking out at the sides.

2 Carefully cut out your glasses, including the holes for the eyes. Fold the arms inwards, and check if your glasses fit you.

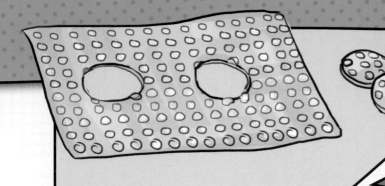

3 On your bubble wrap, draw two circles, the same size as the frames of your glasses. Cut them out.

Another fun idea

With the glasses off, try covering one eye and looking around. Do things look different? Our two eyes give you two slightly different views of the world. This lets you see in 3-D, and judge how far away things are.

4 Glue or tape the bubble wrap circles to the inside of your frames. Once they are firmly in place, try your glasses out!

Try this!

If you can catch a fly in a glass, try looking at it closely. You could use a magnifying glass, if you have one. Can you see its compound eyes?

What has happened?

Flies and many other insects have special eyes called compound eyes. They are made up of lots of mini eyes, all tightly packed together. The fly sees an image of the world divided into small sections – like looking through bubble wrap.

Growing dough

Cut a slice of bread, and you'll see it's full of bubbles. But did you know what makes those bubbles? The answer is: tiny living things.

1 Put the flour, yeast and salt in the bowl. Mix the sugar and 1 tablespoon of oil into the water, then add the water to the flour. Use your hands to mix it together.

2 Shape and squeeze the mixture to make a soft dough. Tip it out onto a table sprinkled with flour, and knead it for 5 minutes.

Tip!
Here's how to knead:
Fold the dough in half.
Press it down with both hands.
Stretch it out a bit sideways.
Fold in half again...
and repeat!

3 Oil the baking sheet. Put your dough on it. Oil the top of the dough, then spread a piece of plastic wrap over it. Leave the dough in a warm place for an hour.

Another fun idea
You can make bread dough into shapes before leaving them to rise. (They will need less cooking time – about 10 minutes.)

4 After an hour, the dough should be much bigger! If you like, you can now bake it in the oven to make bread.

5 Remove the plastic wrap. Preheat the oven to 400°F (200°C). With an adult's help, put the dough in the oven and bake for 30-35 minutes.

6 Carefully take the baked bread out, and leave to cool. When it's ready, cut a slice and look at the bubbles inside.

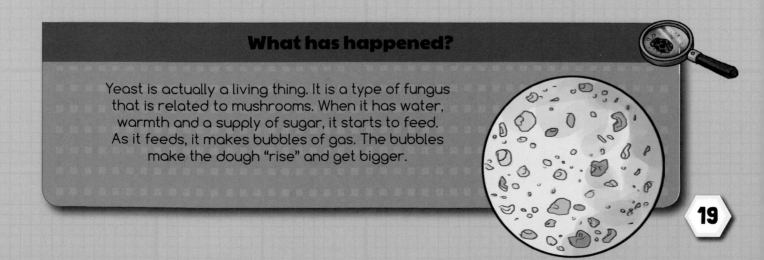

What has happened?

Yeast is actually a living thing. It is a type of fungus that is related to mushrooms. When it has water, warmth and a supply of sugar, it starts to feed. As it feeds, it makes bubbles of gas. The bubbles make the dough "rise" and get bigger.

Mold garden

Mold is a kind of living thing. It is in the fungi family, along with yeast and mushrooms. To see mold growing, grow your own mold garden inside a jar.

You will need:

- Old fruit, old cheese, and stale bread, cake or crackers
- A cooking knife
- A glass jar with a tight-fitting lid
- Adhesive tape
- Water
- Pen and sticky label

1 Chop up your food items into chunks. Sprinkle each one with water, and put them inside the jar.

2 Screw on the lid tightly. Then wrap tape around the edge of the lid too, for an extra-tight seal.

3 Write "Mold Garden - do not open!" on your sticky label, then stick it onto the jar.

4 Put the jar in a safe place where no one will throw it away or play with it.

5 Check the jar every day. Eventually, you should see mold starting to grow on the food.

6 When you've finished with the experiment, throw the jar away, unopened. Mold can be bad for you - it's best not to let it escape.

Try this!
Try looking more closely at the mold with a magnifying glass.
Can you see different types of mold? Can you see little stalks or hairlike parts?

What has happened?

Like mushrooms and toadstools, molds release tiny spores into the air. The spores work like seeds. If they land on food, they can start to grow into new molds. As food starts to get old, mold collects and grows on it.

Mold grows hairs, like tiny roots, into the food to feed on it.

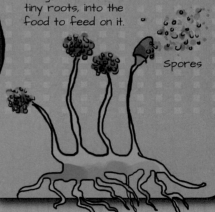

Spores

Spinning pictures

It is easy for your eyes to get confused. If you see things spinning very quickly, they can seem to blend together into one.

1 Cut out a circle of cardboard about 3 inches (8 cm) across. Use the hole punch to make a hole on each side.

2 Cut two pieces of string, then thread one through each hole. Tie each string in a knot to hold it in place.

3 In the middle of the cardboard draw a simple picture, such as a goldfish or a bird. Flip the cardboard over so that it is upside down.

4 Draw another picture on the other side to go with the first picture, such as a goldfish bowl or a cage.

5 Hold the strings on either side of the cardboard, close to the holes. Twist your fingers to make the cardboard spin over and over.

Another fun idea

Here are some more ideas for pictures. Can you think of others too?

Did you know?

This experiment was invented over 150 years ago. In the 1800s, it was called the "thaumatrope."

What has happened?

Your eyes work by detecting patterns of light, and sending signals to your brain. When you see an image, it lasts for a little while in your brain, even if it has disappeared in real life. The spinning cardboard moves so fast that both images end up in your brain at the same time, and seem to get mixed together.

6 As you watch the cardboard spinning, can you see the two pictures appear as one image?

Grabbing hand

Reach out your hand and pretend to grab something. Your fingers curl up towards each other. How do they do that? Find out with this model hand.

You will need:

- Card stock
- Pens
- Scissors
- Straws
- Adhesive tape
- String

1

Draw around your hand and wrist onto the card stock. Cut the shape out using the scissors. Color it in too, if you like!

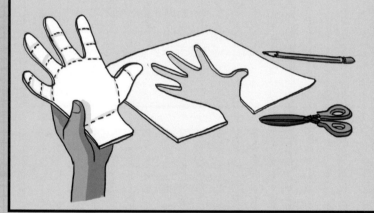

2

On the card stock hand, mark each finger into three sections, like real fingers. Fold the fingers between the sections, like this.

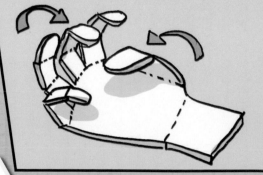

3

Cut pieces of straw slightly shorter than each section. Tape the pieces of straw onto the fingers so that they line up.

4 Tape longer pieces of straw onto the palm of the hand, leading from each finger to the wrist. Make sure they all end at the same place.

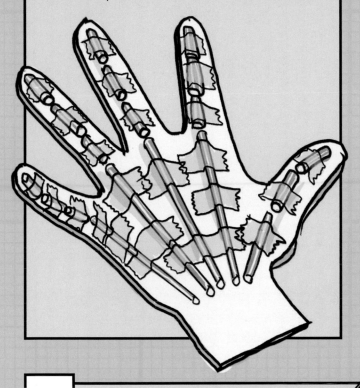

5 Cut five long pieces of string. Thread them through the straws for each finger, and tape them in place at the fingertips.

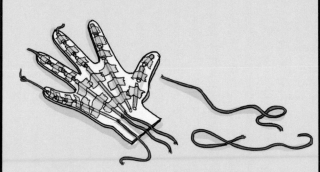

Try this!
Hold your arm tightly about halfway between your wrist and your elbow, and wiggle your fingers. You should be able to feel the muscles and tendons moving.

6 Now hold the hand by the wrist, and gently pull on the string. Your hand will curl up and grab, just like a real one!

Did you know?
Many animals have body parts that work the same way – like a chicken's foot or a tiger's paw.

What has happened?

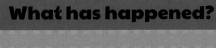

Your body contains muscles that make you move by pulling on your bones. The muscles that move your fingers are in your arms. They are connected to stringy parts called tendons that connect to your fingers.

Blink reflex

A reflex is something your body does by itself, without you deciding to do it. Reflexes can be useful, as they help to protect us.

You will need:

- A door with a glass window in it, or a ground-floor window
- Cotton balls
- Two or more people

1 One person should stand behind the glass, with their face up close to it and their eyes wide open.

2 Another person should stand on the other side of the glass, and throw cotton balls at the first person's face, one at a time.

3 The first person has to try not to blink. When they've had a turn, swap places. It's very hard to keep your eyes open!

Did you know?
Your blink reflex protects your eyes from dangers like flying sand or insects.

What has happened?

Your blink reflex makes your eyes shut if anything moves quickly towards your face. Even though you know the glass is in the way, it's very hard to stop your eyes from shutting.

Food tubes

When you eat food, it goes into your stomach, then travels through a long set of tubes called intestines. Let's find out how long they are!

1 First, ask someone to measure how tall you are. Write down the results on your paper.

51 inches (130 cm)

2 Use the calculator to multiply your height by five. Write down the answer on the paper.

51 in (130 cm) × 5 =

3 The answer shows how long your intestines are! Measure out a piece of string that long.

What has happened?

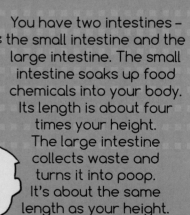

You have two intestines – the small intestine and the large intestine. The small intestine soaks up food chemicals into your body. Its length is about four times your height. The large intestine collects waste and turns it into poop. It's about the same length as your height.

Your intestines are coiled up in loops and folds. That's how they fit inside you!

Plants need light and water to grow - so when there's not enough rain, it can be a disaster for crop farmers. This farmer's corn has failed to grow properly after a drought.

Calcium makes bones strong - but they do sometimes break, as you can see in this X-ray. Luckily, our bones can mend themselves by growing new bone across the break.

All living things need food - and that means they eat each other. Zebras are plant eaters. This zebra is being stalked by a lion, a hunter that eats other animals.

When you watch a film, it looks as if everything is moving. In fact, you're seeing a sequence of pictures, one after another, very fast. Your brain blends the pictures together to look like a moving image.

29

Further information

Books

Amazing Science: Plants by Sally Hewitt (Wayland, 2014)

Big Bang Science Experiments: It's Alive! The Science of Plants and Living Things by Jay Hawkins (Windmill Books, 2013)

Living Things by Anna Claybourne (Wayland, 2015)

Read and Experiment: Experiments with Plants by Isabel Thomas (Raintree, 2015)

Websites

For web resources related to the subject of this book, go to: **www.windmillbooks.com/weblinks** and select this book's title.

Glossary

calcium
A mineral that strengthens bones in the body.

dissolve
The process of a solid mixing with a liquid and becoming liquid.

drought
A long period of dry weather that can be damaging to crops.

germ
A type of microorganism, especially one that causes illness and disease.

intestines
The small intestine and the large intestine are long tubes that food passes through. They are part of the digestive system.

knead
To work a material, like dough or clay, into a uniform mixture by folding and stretching.

microorganism
A living creature that is too small for us to see with the naked eye, such as a bacterium.

mold
A fungus that grows on damp or decaying matter.

rubbery
Something that is bendy like rubber or elastic.

species
A group of living things that resemble each other and have shared characteristics.

spore
A reproductive cell that grows into a new plant, found on ferns and molds.

tendon
A band of connective tissue that attaches muscles to bones.

tripod
A three-legged stand or support for a camera.

yeast
A fungus used as an ingredient in bread to make it expand.

Index